$7

D1372136

ZODICAT
Speaks

ZODICAT
Speaks

by Doctor Zodicat

*Discover
Your Cat's
Astrological
Signature*

A Wuthering Book **VIKING**

VIKING
Published by the Penguin Group
Penguin Books USA Inc., 375 Hudson Street, New York, New York 10014, U.S.A.
Penguin Books Ltd, 27 Wrights Lane, London W8 5TZ, England
Penguin Books Australia Ltd, Ringwood, Victoria, Australia
Penguin Books Canada Ltd, 10 Alcorn Avenue, Toronto, Ontario, Canada M4V 3B2
Penguin Books (N.Z.) Ltd, 182–190 Wairau Road, Auckland 10, New Zealand

Penguin Books Ltd, Registered Offices: Harmondsworth, Middlesex, England

First published in 1996 by Viking Penguin, a division of Penguin Books USA Inc.

10 9 8 7 6 5 4 3 2 1

Copyright © A.S.A. Harrison, 1996
Illustrations copyright © Wesley W. Bates, 1996
All rights reserved

ISBN 0-670-86858-2
CIP data is available from the Library of Congress.

This book is printed on acid-free paper. ∞

Printed in the United States of America
Set in 12 pt Weiss
Designed by Christine Higdon (Goodness Graphics), Toronto

If you haven't a clue when your cat was born, take heart. I have written this book with you in mind. Humans being what they are (busy, stressed-out, not very intuitive), I wanted to make it ultra-simple for you to guess your cat's Sun sign. You'll be amazed at how easy it is. Start with the mini-questionnaire on the next page, then check your best guesses in the chapters that follow. If you do happen to know kitty's birth date, just look through these pages to find the corresponding sign.

Astrologically, the Sun represents innermost essence or divine nature, while the twelve signs of the Zodiac, from Aries to Pisces, symbolize a range of attitudes. Thus, the sign through which the Sun was passing at the time of birth, known as the Sun sign, provides a key to personality. Sun signs don't give you the whole story, but they do indicate the strongest character traits and most basic underlying motives.

Anyone who is familiar with felines knows that, like humans, each of us possesses a distinct personality and bestows unique blessings on those around us. As astrology helps you to understand yourself, so it can reveal many of your cat's best-kept secrets. *Meow.*

Three Easy Steps to Guessing Your Cat's Sun Sign

 Decide if your cat has a cardinal, fixed, or mutable approach to life. (Check one.)

❍ **Cardinal**   Insistent, assertive, gets things going

❍ **Fixed**   Persevering, obstinate, dogged

❍ **Mutable**   Flexible, capricious, manipulative

2 **Decide if your cat has a fire, earth, air, or water personality.** (Check one.)

❍ **Fire**   Proud, demonstrative, adventurous

❍ **Earth**   Sensuous, self-centered, comfort-seeking

❍ **Air**   Observant, talkative, aloof

❍ **Water**   Sensitive, impressionable, temperamental

3 **Look up your cat's sign on the chart.**

	Cardinal	Fixed	Mutable
Fire	Aries	Leo	Sagittarius
Earth	Capricorn	Taurus	Virgo
Air	Libra	Aquarius	Gemini
Water	Cancer	Scorpio	Pisces

Still undecided? Read on.

— Dr. Zodicat

Aries

March 20/21 to April 19/20

Mode: **Cardinal**

Element: **Fire**

Rulership: **Mars**

Ruled by warlike Mars, Aries is the most dynamic and forthright of all the signs. Firebrands as kittens, Aries felines blossom into bullies and daredevils by early adolescence. Driven by their lust for excitement and (mis)adventure, they always have somewhere to go and something to do. They can be hugely affectionate and purr like thunder (fire signs do it the loudest) – but only when it suits them. The secret with Ariens is this: you play their game, by their rules.

Aptitudes

- Finding the shortest distance between two points
- Any thoughtless, impulsive act
- As kittens: hunting and slaughtering rolled-up socks
- As adults: roaming the neighborhood looking for trouble
- At all stages of life: waiting in ambush, hand-to-hand combat, narrow escapes

A Attitudes

- Prefer sleeping outside (if deprived of this pleasure will snooze in doorways – the better to swipe at your ankles when you pass)
- Take all nine of their lives into their own hands
- Believe that the world is their oyster
- Would say if they could: "I did it my way."

Big Red

CASE STUDY

An unusually fierce ginger tabby, Big Red enjoys breaking into the house of a neighboring calico cat. He enters by ripping a hole in the window screen and, once inside, holds the poor little calico hostage. Eventually the humans return and chase Big Red out of the house with a broom. Undaunted, Red pauses on the doorstep, grins maniacally, and hisses, as if to say: "I'll be back."

Zodicat's Guide to Aries

Life Ambition: To rule the roost

Pet Peeve: Upstarts

Favorite Pastime: Going anywhere

Ultimate Pleasure: Showing up days later

Moment of Truth: Locked out

Highest Expression of Love: Coming home at all

Karmic Downfall: Birds perched on balcony railings

Traumatic Past-Life Experience: A fifth-floor balcony

Possible Professions: Warrior, feminist

Appropriate Names: Bodicea, Genghis, King Kong, Germaine

Taurus

April 20/21 to May 20/21

Mode: **Fixed**

Element: **Earth**

Rulership: **Venus**

Taurus is the classic cat: lazy, sensuous, independent, and obstinate. Did someone say obstinate? Let's just say that Taurus is the Zodiac's immovable force. Try to budge this cat against its will and you will have to try, try again. But neither can you stand in the way of a Taurus with a plan. Grooming is terribly important to these felines. Not only does it feel good – it makes the coat shine. With seductive Venus as their ruler, vain, complacent Taureans know they are lovelier in every way than other cats.

Aptitudes

- Watching your sandwich as it travels between your plate and your mouth
- Insisting on endless games of fetch with tin-foil balls or screwed-up fax paper (you are likely to find an assortment of these in your bed each morning)
- Drinking an entire pitcher of cream, drop by drop, from a curled paw (it may take hours)
- Walking around with tail pointing straight up in the air

Attitudes

- Understand that beauty is only skin deep
- Enjoy sitting in the laps of visitors (preferably of the opposite sex)
- Can't be diverted from above indulgence (hop back on when pushed off)
- Avoid rugs and chairs that clash with their coloring
- Wouldn't dream of coming when called

Flo

CASE STUDY

A fluffy tabby with an immaculate white ruff, Flo keeps herself beautifully groomed at all times. She has to — her human is a photographer who always has several loaded cameras lying around. Whenever he picks one up, Flo immediately assumes a dignified posture and gazes into the lens. The human has tried, but failed, to capture a single variation on this pose.

Zodicat's Guide to Taurus

Life Ambition: To find a really reliable hairdresser

Pet Peeve: Getting caught in the rain

Favorite Pastime: Sleeping through crises

Ultimate Pleasure: Scratching flea bites when no one is looking

Moment of Truth: Caught with a milk mustache

Highest Expression of Love: Primping and preening in front of you

Karmic Downfall: All those extra tidbits

Traumatic Past-Life Experience: Not photogenic

Possible Professions: Epicure, voluptuary

Appropriate Names: Escoffier, Bacchus, Julia, Isadora

Gemini

May 21/22 to June 20/21
Mode: **Mutable**
Element: **Air**
Rulership: **Mercury**

Whoever said that *curiosity killed the cat* was surely talking about a Gemini, though in Gemini's case *curious* is just a polite way of saying *nosy*. These cats are what you might call Peeping Toms. A mutable sign, versatile Gemini actually enjoys wearing clothes, and may be the only cat on record to hop into the tub at bath time. Capricious and agile, Geminians are the dancers and acrobats of the feline world. Ruled by restless Mercury, these busybodies are constantly active, seemingly tireless, easily awakened, and can't go to sleep if something – anything – is afoot.

Aptitudes
- Sudden, gravity-defying movements (backflips, somersaults, vertical leaps from all fours)
- The hundred-yard dash across the carpet (turns into a skid on bare floor)
- Banking around corners, as in Roller Derby
- Opening doors
- Being in the wrong place at the wrong time

Attitudes

- Not team players
- Tend to pester playmates (follow them around, bat at their tails, steal their toys) – naturally it's all in good fun
- Happy to interact with any species (things don't work out too well for canaries and goldfish)
- Think other signs are slow and dull-witted

Chico

Though aging and overweight, Chico takes a daily constitutional as follows: races out of the house to the end of the yard, looks both ways, does a lively dance on his hind legs, then races back in. Variation: runs out sideways and runs back with the opposite side leading.

Zodicat's Guide to Gemini

Life Ambition: To be where the action is

Pet Peeve: Locked doors

Favorite Pastimes: Trying on new outfits, snooping into everyone else's affairs

Ultimate Pleasure: Eavesdropping

Moment of Truth: Caught eavesdropping

Highest Expression of Love: Four-point landing on object of affection

Karmic Downfall: Accidental destruction of playmates

Traumatic Past-Life Experience: Was bored once

Possible Professions: Dancer, spy

Appropriate Names: Nijinsky, Fred'n'Ginger, Mata Hari, 007

Cancer

June 21/22 to July 22/23
Mode: **Cardinal**
Element: **Water**
Rulership: **Moon**

You never know quite what to expect from a Cancer cat. These odd-balls seem to crave attention and sympathy, yet they routinely spend long hours holed up where no one can find them. Though often crabby themselves, they hate to be reprimanded, and may even run away when scolded. Cancerians can be feisty and aggressive, but Moon rulership gives them a sensitive, sentimental side – they enjoy being pampered and babied. Add to this a talent for comical antics and you have a most complex and unpredictable cat.

Aptitudes

- Glaring at you from a corner of the room
- Breaking into a spontaneous impersonation of a happy, playful cat (Cancer may suddenly notice the toy mouse that's been lying on the floor all winter, torment it with gleeful abandon for three minutes, then go on ignoring it for the rest of the year)
- Taking the most circuitous route imaginable to get anywhere
- Walking directly across your path several times a day

Attitudes

- ◆ Attracted to mother figures – prone to infantile behavior (kneading and sucking)
- ◆ Incapable of taking direct action (when craving solitude, for example, may take offense at some insignificant slight, thus finding reason to stalk off)
- ◆ Plagued by feelings of insecurity – lay their catch at your feet, hoping that you'll freeze it for the coming food shortage

Portia

CASE STUDY

Portia, a fat Persian also known as the Bearded Lady, sometimes disappears on Friday, then shows up for dinner on Sunday as if nothing unusual has happened. This behavior fulfills two important needs: it satisfies her love of solitude, and serves as a nicely roundabout way to get attention – from her hiding place, Portia can hear her humans calling her name all weekend long.

Zodicat's Guide to Cancer

Life Ambition: Who can tell?

Pet Peeve: Being misunderstood

Favorite Pastime: Brooding

Ultimate Pleasure: Making a scene

Moment of Truth: Not taken seriously

Highest Expression of Love: Forgiving you eventually

Karmic Downfall: Lingering grudges

Traumatic Past-Life Experience: Mummified

Possible Professions: Clown, drama queen

Appropriate Names: Neon, Clarabel, Liz, Divine

Leo

July 23/24 to August 22/23
Mode: **Fixed**
Element: **Fire**
Rulership: **Sun**

Leo cats have warm, sunny dispositions and magnetic personalities. People gravitate towards these Sun-ruled cats and remark on their natural radiance. The overriding trait of Leos is their insatiable craving for admiration. Don't be fooled by the quiet ones – they are just as adept at attracting notice as the showy, outspoken Leos. This spirited fire sign hungers for outdoor adventure, but looks forward to getting home. After all, home is where the audience is.

Aptitudes

- A flair for the dramatic – a Leo who wants a second breakfast falls across your feet and looks up at you plaintively (Oliver Twist at the orphanage, feline rendition)
- Working hard to achieve their goals – a Leo who wants to go outside paces the room like a lion at the zoo, giving that precise impression of cruel and unjust imprisonment (if you are heartless enough to ignore this behavior, Leo simply darts between your legs when you open the door for the mail carrier)
- Relaxing in the Sphinx position (they've seen it on TV)

A Attitudes

- Happily entertain your guests – keen to impress newcomers (Leo doesn't stand on formalities)
- Too dignified to play with toys – watch with an air of benevolent disinterest while the other cats indulge
- Attracted to people who wear perfume and jewelry
- Bear up bravely when their pride is hurt

Duke

CASE STUDY

Duke likes to entertain guests by parading in front of them carrying a feather-duster in his mouth. They love it. He swaggers across the room with this splendid prop, then exits by the hall door. Seconds later, he's back, booty still in tow. Now he crosses the room in the other direction, and disappears through the opposite door. People cheer and call his name. Will there be an encore? Yes! As long as his public needs him, Duke goes on with the show – a Leo in his element, making entrance after entrance.

Zodicat's Guide to Leo

Life Ambition: To have the floor

Pet Peeve: Other Leos

Favorite Pastime: Working an audience

Ultimate Pleasure: Lapping up flattery

Moment of Truth: Catcalls

Highest Expression of Love: Effusive displays of good will

Karmic Downfall: Trying anything once

Traumatic Past-Life Experience: Played second fiddle

Possible Professions: Performer, show-off

Appropriate Names: Diva, Dolly, Olivier, Mick

Virgo

August 23/24 to September 22/23
Mode: **Mutable**
Element: **Earth**
Rulership: **Mercury**

If you want something done, don't hesitate to ask a Virgo, even a Virgo cat. Ruled by fidgety Mercury (like Gemini), this sign is forever busy. Virgo's specialty is rendering service to others, with a focus on detail – the small tasks, the daily round of chores. Virgos are also sensuous and romantic – smells and textures delight them, and they are quick to win your heart with their thoughtful gestures. These cats may be shy around strangers, but are easily enticed out of hiding by a favorite toy. Play – to a Virgo cat – is *almost* as much fun as work.

Aptitudes

- Tidying the litter box after the other cats have used it
- Bringing tiny treasures in from outdoors (twigs, pebbles, bits of organic matter)
- Fertilizing the garden (in good weather, these helpful cats abandon the litter box altogether)
- Gnawing on toy mice till they are pulpy and soaked with saliva – thoughtfully leaving these choice objects in your shoe (along with the occasional real dead mouse)

Attitudes

- Enjoy playing with anything small and chewy (wee rubber balls, woolly bits, assorted bugs)
- Take play seriously
- Think they know best, having perfected a system for doing almost everything
- Worry a lot, and feel overly responsible

Diana

CASE STUDY

This lovely Virgo Siamese does a daily round of chores that includes licking spills off the kitchen floor and nosing around the carpet like a miniature vacuum cleaner, sucking up all the bits of stuff that make a mess (crumbs, lint, dead flies). Diana frequently turns up her nose at her dinner but will eat almost anything else in the interests of good housekeeping.

Zodicat's Guide to Virgo

Life Ambition: To stay at home and get some work done

Pet Peeve: Running out of chores

Favorite Pastime: Licking your fingers (tastes good *and* helps you out)

Ultimate Pleasure: Smelling your breath (Yumm.)

Moment of Truth: Caught relaxing

Highest Expression of Love: Worrying

Karmic Downfall: Overextended

Traumatic Past-Life Experience: A bovine existence

Possible Professions: Butler, housekeeper

Appropriate Names: Jeeves, Friday, Hazel, (Mrs.) Hudson

Libra

September 23/24 to October 22/23

Mode: **Cardinal**

Element: **Air**

Rulership: **Venus**

Charm is Libra's whole way of life. This graceful, seductive, diplomatic feline knows how to flatter you, amuse you, and make you feel special. But don't be too dazzled by Libra's adoring gazes and perky amiability. Libra is a cardinal sign, and that means pushy, even though in Libra's case it's honey coated. Libran cats become devoted to their humans, expect love and appreciation in return, and will do almost anything to get them.

Aptitudes

- Sitting patiently at the window, watching for your return
- Greeting you with genuine delight
- Looking beautiful – Venus rulership (which they share with Taurus) makes them vain, keeps them well groomed, and puts a strut in their walk
- Inventing ever-more-devious ways to get your attention
- Running your life

Attitudes

- Need to believe that you are constantly thinking of them
- Like to receive expensive gifts (gourmet food, decorative collars, silk pillows)
- May refuse to speak to you when you've been away on a trip, but can't keep up the silent treatment for long (Scorpio holds the record)
- Pride themselves on being very *nice* cats

Goldfinger

CASE STUDY

Although he feels that he and his human should be spending more time together, Goldfinger wouldn't dream of making unreasonable demands. When his tail falls across her computer screen, when he steps on her TV remote and accidentally changes channels, when he unwittingly walks on her crossword puzzle — well, these are honest mistakes. After all, when friends visit, Goldfinger sits with his back politely turned — so as not to intrude.

Zodicat's Guide to Libra

Life Ambition: Keeping up appearances

Pet Peeves: Your job, your friends, your hobbies

Favorite Pastime: Having your undivided attention

Ultimate Pleasure: Having your undivided attention while others watch

Moment of Truth: Hearing their name taken in vain

Highest Expression of Love: Keeping you on a short leash

Karmic Downfall: Resorting to ultimatums

Traumatic Past-Life Experience: Loved and lost

Possible Professions: Diplocat, consort

Appropriate Names: Scheherezade, Prince Albert, Potemkin, Pompadour

Scorpio

October 23/24 to November 21/22

Mode: **Fixed**

Element: **Water**

Rulership: **Pluto**

This is the cat most likely to develop stubborn obsessions, great loves, and lasting aversions. Emotionally retentive Scorpions are deeply passionate, yet Pluto rulership gives them a cold, controlling side. Silent and secretive, they create rituals around all they do. These are the most possessive cats in the Zodiac – once you have won their devotion, they begin to monitor your routines. Scorpio cats know exactly what you should be doing at all times, and expect you to be prompt. If you're late, or even early, they become confused and angry.

Aptitudes

- Showing up at two minutes to meal time (most cats have excellent internal clocks, but Scorpions have internal stopwatches)
- Behaving obsessively around food – gorging on pizza, or lying on the floor with head in the food bowl, nibbling (if this cat were a person, she'd be on the sofa in a black slip, eating chocolates)
- Unnerving you with silent, intense gazes

Attitudes

♦ Dislike being fondled, picked up, or addressed in baby-talk

♦ Can't help being catty (waiting under the bed to attack the feet of your paramour, peeing in your suitcase when you're packing for a trip)

♦ Spend most of their time seething with passion (anger, jealousy, desire), yet give a convincing impression of icy indifference

Larry

CASE STUDY

In his callow years, Larry fell in love with a ginger cat called Vanessa, who lived in an adjacent apartment. During the summer of his passion, Larry spent long days and nights camped out on Vanessa's balcony. Desperate to get a look at her, he climbed onto her screen door and hung there for hours. Vanessa ignored him, but Larry never gave up. Now in his golden years, Larry continues to honor his first love. Ginger females are the only cats allowed on his property.

Zodicat's Guide to Scorpio

Life Ambition: To find a soul mate

Pet Peeves: Clocks that run slow, people who break promises

Favorite Pastime: Falling in love

Ultimate Pleasure: Getting even

Moment of Truth: Falling in love again

Highest Expression of Love: Jealous rages

Karmic Downfall: Secret enemies

Traumatic Past-Life Experience: They called it puppy love

Possible Profession: Cat

Appropriate Names: Sylvester, Fritz, Dinah, Bastet

Sagittarius

November 22/23 to December 21/22
Mode: **Mutable**
Element: **Fire**
Rulership: **Jupiter**

Ruled by expansive Jupiter, Sagittarians take great pleasure in cultivating a wide circle of friends – including everyone from your sister's dog to the nice man who delivered flyers last week. This is the cat who waits on the sidewalk to greet everyone who strolls by – the one-cat, neighborhood good-will committee. Some say Sagittarians are hustlers and entrepreneurs, but cats of this sign have a naive and optimistic nature that leaves them best suited to being the life of the party.

Aptitudes

- Behaving like a human (standing on hind legs at the table to watch you eat, placing a paw in your hand, wrapping both arms around your neck when picked up)
- Interacting with your head (bonking foreheads, rubbing noses, wrestling with your hair, lying on your face)
- Hanging over the TV screen to see what's on
- Bringing strays home to dinner

Attitudes

- Candid and tactless (but friendly)
- Willing to give absolutely anybody a chance
- Believe that life is one great adventure
- Enjoy contact sports and group games (hockey, wrestling, tag, soccer, volleyball)
- Think of the bathtub as a combination rink, ring, court, and stadium

Tic-Tac

CASE STUDY

When this Sagittarian visited the vet recently, she was admittedly nervous about getting her shots, but even this couldn't dampen her exuberant spirits. While on the examining table, she leapt to her feet, put her front paws on the vet's shoulder, and gave him a cordial lick on the chin. Sagittarian motto: Never overlook an opportunity to make a new friend, even one with a hypodermic needle.

Zodicat's Guide to Sagittarius

Life Ambition: To make as many friends as possible

Pet Peeve: Misanthropes

Favorite Pastime: Schmoozing

Ultimate Pleasure: Any vigorous activity

Moment of Truth: Reduced to tail chasing

Highest Expression of Love: Holding hands

Karmic Downfall: Taking democracy to extremes

Traumatic Past-Life Experience: None known

Possible Professions: Co-pilot, sidekick

Appropriate Names: Josephine, Lady Bird, Tonto, Dr. Watson

Capricorn

December 22/23 to January 19/20

Mode: **Cardinal**

Element: **Earth**

Rulership: **Saturn**

When your Capricorn cat is stretched out with eyes half-closed – beware. This brilliant schemer is not innocently dozing. Saturn-ruled Capricorns are the empire builders of the Zodiac. Ambitious and circumspect, they crave power and prestige and know how to get them: careful planning followed by aggressive action. These cats respect authority because they want it themselves, and so contrive to use rules and protocol to get the upper hand. Knowing just what's going to happen next is what gives Capricorn cats their edge.

Aptitudes

- Using clever strategies to defend the home front (example: climbing into the garage rafters to await marauding felines – teaching them a lesson they won't forget)
- Sleeping with their front ends facing one way and their back ends facing the other way, just to confuse you
- Cat-and-mouse games
- Fooling you without your ever knowing it

Attitudes

- ◆ Dote on bodily rites and pleasures – lick themselves noisily, snore loudly when sleeping, curl their toes when scratched between the shoulder blades
- ◆ Want more out of life than other cats, and go at things with extra drive
- ◆ Feel that bending rules is not the same as breaking them
- ◆ Believe that ends justify means

Barky

CASE STUDY

An innocent human was driving to work one morning, and had just turned onto the freeway, when the knapsack she had placed on the seat beside her started to wriggle and squirm. A moment later, her cat Barky poked his head out, taking her totally by surprise and more or less ruining her morning. From Barky's point of view, showing his human who's really in charge was well worth the hours of planning and the long wait in that stuffy knapsack.

Zodicat's Guide to Capricorn

Life Ambition: To have the upper hand

Pet Peeve: Being a cat

Favorite Pastime: Feigning cat-like interests

Ultimate Pleasure: Secretly studying human behavior

Moment of Truth: Outsmarted

Highest Expression of Love: Simulating obedience

Karmic Downfall: Stress

Traumatic Past-Life Experience: Played the fool

Possible Profession: Politician

Appropriate Names: Winston, Machiavelli, Indira, Cleopatra

Aquarius

January 20/21 to February 18/19

Mode: **Fixed**

Element: **Air**

Rulership: **Uranus**

Aquarian cats are cool, aloof, and impersonal. Combine this with their need to inspect everyone they come across, of whatever species, and you have the cat most likely to get into trouble. These cats are seekers who feel compelled to find out what you (and others) are made of. Aquarian *humans* ask a lot of questions; Aquarian *felines* search your soul with their eyes. Their interest is genuine – but don't expect it to last. This elitist cat bonds with a select few and regards all others as curiosities.

Aptitudes

- Walking straight up to dogs to get a really good look at them
- Keeping a file on you
- Giving you looks (a fast once-over, a sidelong glance, a rude stare)
- Making definitive statements (on the carpet, in the car), but only with good reason

Attitudes

- Gravitate to crowds (not because they're friendly but because they get to check out a lot of people all at once)
- Delight in strange and exotic foods – willing to try almost anything
- Relish a good argument (remain cool and unruffled while opponents rant and rave – or scratch and bite)
- Grow increasingly eccentric with age

Gertrude & Alice

CASE STUDY

Aquarian kittens, Gertrude and Alice, who killed a squirrel at the tender age of four-and-a-half months, were not really hunting the squirrel. They just went along to investigate, maybe take a few notes. Their surprised humans found them standing on top of the vanquished animal, pulling out tufts of its hair with their teeth. G & A are sorry about the accident, but keen to learn more.

Zodicat's Guide to Aquarius

Life Ambition: To understand the secrets of the universe

Pet Peeve: People who wear sunglasses

Favorite Pastime: Observing while unobserved

Ultimate Pleasure: Arguing fine points

Moment of Truth: Caught sharpening their nails

Highest Expression of Love: Tossing you an appreciative glance

Karmic Downfall: Taking too theoretical an approach to life

Traumatic Past-Life Experience: Unwanted intimacy

Possible Professions: Sleuth, reporter

Appropriate Names: Nick, Nora, Nancy, Marlowe

Pisces

February 19/20 to March 19/20

Mode: **Mutable**

Element: **Water**

Rulership: **Neptune**

Pisces and Aries are adjacent signs, yet they couldn't have less in common. The first and last signs of the Zodiac, they represent the beginning and end of the life cycle. Aries is like the newborn, brimming with untamed impulses, whereas Pisces is the sage – compassionate, wise, and empathic. This is the pet that senses your feelings, reflects your mood, and offers you comfort when you're feeling blue. Pisceans do, however, have ideas of their own. Ruled by fanciful Neptune, they are dreamers who live in an enchanted world that few can enter.

Aptitudes

- Turning banal circumstance into full-blooded drama – the fur along a Piscean spine can go rigid at the spectre of a mark on the floor (on a good day, a Piscean back goes up at the sight of the floor itself)
- Staring at walls
- Staring at corners
- Giving you a good scolding when you need it

Attitudes

- Disapprove if they catch you feeling sorry for yourself
- Believe that life is brief and should be filled with as much light-hearted play as possible
- Consider their visions and fantasies to be as real as anything else
- When hunting, do not distinguish rubber bands and cellophane from mice
- Regard themselves as figments of their own imagination

Taeko

CASE STUDY

This mostly white calico refused to walk on the new living-room carpet for weeks after it arrived. She sat in the doorway staring at the carpet, then glancing at the ceiling, apparently fearing that another carpet would come crashing down from above. Some say Piscean cats are timid, but the truth is that, in their wisdom, they know enough to be cautious around the spirits who live in the woodwork.

Zodicat's Guide to Pisces

Life Ambition: None

Pet Peeve: Missing a nap

Favorite Pastime: Chasing shadows

Ultimate Pleasure: Dozing off

Moment of Truth: Waking up

Highest Expression of Love: Total identification with the loved one

Karmic Downfall: Reality

Traumatic Past-Life Experience: Forced to hunt for food

Possible Professions: Mystic, martyr, healer

Appropriate Names: Gandhi, Sebastian, Joan, Tammy-Faye

The End